Glory Be

Glory and to th ginning, is now, end. Amen.

The Angelus

The Angel of the Lord declared unto Mary.
And she conceived of the Holy Spirit.
Hail Mary, etc.
Behold the handmaid of the Lord.
May it be done unto me according to your word.
Hail Mary, etc.
And the Word was made flesh.
And dwelt among us.
Hail Mary, etc.
V. Pray for us, O Holy Mother of God.
R. That we may be made worthy of the promises of Christ.
 Let us pray - O Lord, it was through the message of an angel that we learned of the incarnation of your Son Christ. Pour your grace into our hearts, and by his passion and cross bring us to the glory of his resurrection. Through the same Christ, our Lord. Amen.
 Glory be to the Father, etc.

The Apostles' Creed

 I believe in God, the Father Almighty, Creator of heaven and earth; and in Jesus Christ,

His only Son, our Lord; who was conceived by the Holy Spirit, born of the Virgin Mary, suffered under Pontius Pilate, was crucified, died and was buried. He descended into hell; the third day He arose again from the dead; He ascended into heaven, sits at the right hand of God, the Father Almighty; from thence He shall come to judge the living and the dead. I believe in the Holy Spirit, the Holy Catholic Church, the communion of saints, the forgiveness of sins, the resurrection of the body, and life everlasting. Amen.

An Act of Faith

O my God, I firmly believe that You are one God in three Divine Persons, Father, Son, and Holy Spirit; I believe that Your Divine Son became man and died for our sins, and that He will come to judge the living and the dead. I believe these and all the truths which the Holy Catholic Church teaches, because You revealed them, who can neither deceive nor be deceived.

An Act of Hope

O my God, relying on Your infinite goodness and promises, I hope to obtain pardon of my sins, the help of Your grace, and life everlasting, through the merits of Jesus Christ, my Lord and Redeemer.

An Act of Love

O my God, I love You above all things, with my whole heart and soul, because You are all-good and worthy of all love. I love my neighbor as myself for the love of You. I forgive all who have injured me, and I ask pardon of all whom I have injured.

An Act of Contrition

O my God, I am heartily sorry for having offended You, and I detest all my sins, because of Your just punishments, but most of all because they offend You, my God, who are all-good and deserving of all my love. I firmly resolve, with the help of Your grace, to sin no more and to avoid the near occasions of sin.

Morning Offering

O Jesus, through the Immaculate Heart of Mary, I offer You all my prayers, works, joys and sufferings of this day, for all the intentions of Your Sacred Heart, in union with the Holy Sacrifice of the Mass throughout the world, in reparation for my sins, for the intentions of all our associates, and for the general intention recommended this month.

Prayer Before Meals

Bless us, O Lord, and these Your gifts, which we are to receive from Your bounty, through Christ our Lord. Amen.

Prayer After Meals

We give You thanks for all Your benefits, O almighty God, who lives and reigns forever; and may the souls of the faithful departed, through the mercy of God, rest in peace. Amen.

Prayer Before a Crucifix

Behold, my beloved and good Jesus, I cast myself upon my knees in Your sight, and with the most fervent desire of my soul I pray and beseech You to impress upon my heart lively sentiments of faith, hope and charity, with true repentance for my sins and a most firm desire of amendment; while with deep affection and grief of soul I consider within myself and mentally contemplate Your five most precious wounds, having before my eyes that which David, the prophet, long ago spoke about You, my Jesus:
"They have pierced my hands and my feet;
I can count all my bones" (Ps. 22:17-18).

Hail, Holy Queen

Hail, holy Queen, Mother of Mercy, our life, our sweetness, and our hope! To you we cry, poor banished children of Eve; to you we send up our sighs, mourning and weeping in this valley of tears. Turn then, O most gracious advocate, your eyes of mercy toward us, and after this our exile, show unto us the blessed fruit of your womb, Jesus. O clement, O loving, O sweet Virgin Mary.

Memorare

Remember, O most gracious Virgin Mary, that never was it known that anyone who fled to your protection, implored your assistance or sought your intercession, was left unaided. Inspired with this confidence, we fly to you, O Virgin of virgins, our Mother; to you we come; before you we kneel, sinful and sorrowful. O Mother of the Word Incarnate, despise not our petitions, but in your clemency hear and answer them. Amen.

How To Say the Rosary

The complete rosary consists of fifteen decades, but it is divided into three distinct parts, each containing five decades. The first part is called the *Five Joyful Mysteries*, the second part the *Five Sorrowful Mysteries*, and the third part the *Five Glorious Mysteries*.

We begin the rosary by blessing ourselves with the crucifix and saying at the same time: "Incline unto my aid, O God; O Lord, make haste to help me."

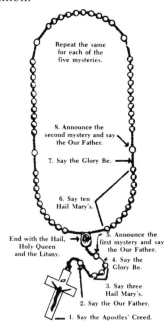

Repeat the same for each of the five mysteries.

8. Announce the second mystery and say the Our Father.

7. Say the Glory Be.

6. Say ten Hail Mary's.

End with the Hail, Holy Queen and the Litany.

5. Announce the first mystery and say the Our Father.

4. Say the Glory Be.

3. Say three Hail Mary's.

2. Say the Our Father.

1. Say the Apostles' Creed.

Then we may say the "Apostles' Creed," one "Our Father," three "Hail Mary's" and one "Glory be to the Father" on the small chain. It is not necessary to say these prayers in order to gain the indulgences connected with the rosary.

The following is necessary: Meditate on the mystery, say one "Our Father" and ten "Hail Mary's." This completes one decade, and all the other decades are said in the same manner with a different mystery meditated during each decade. Each decade is customarily concluded with a "Glory be to the Father." At the end of the rosary the "Hail, Holy Queen" and the Litany of the Blessed Virgin may be recited.

The Mysteries of the Rosary

These mysteries — which present themselves as scenes, pictures and stories, one after another — lead you to an intellectual vision of the facts of the life of Jesus and Mary recorded in the mysteries, and to an understanding of the most sublime truths of our religion: the incarnation of the Lord, the redemption, and the Christian life, present and future. —POPE PAUL VI

Joyful Mysteries (MON. AND THURS.)

1. Annunciation of the Angel to Mary (*Humility*)
2. Mary's Visit to Her Cousin Elizabeth (*Love of Neighbor*)
3. Birth of Jesus in the Stable of Bethlehem (*Spirit of Poverty*)
4. Presentation of Jesus in the Temple (*Obedience to God's Will*)
5. Jesus Is Found Again among the Doctors in the Temple (*Fidelity to Vocation*)

Sorrowful Mysteries (TUES. AND FRI.)

1. Jesus Prays at Gethsemane (*Spirit of Prayer*)
2. Jesus Is Scourged at the Pillar (*Modesty*)
3. Jesus Is Crowned with Thorns (*Purity of Mind and Heart*)

4. Jesus Carries the Cross to Calvary *(Patience in Suffering)*
5. Jesus Dies for Our Sins *(Love for the Mass)*

Glorious Mysteries   (WED., SAT. AND SUN.)
1. Jesus Rises from the Dead *(Faith)*
2. Jesus Ascends into Heaven *(Desire for Heaven)*
3. The Holy Spirit Descends on the Apostles *(Wisdom, Fortitude, Zeal)*
4. The Mother of Jesus Is Assumed into Heaven *(Holy Life, Holy Death)*
5. Mary is Crowned Queen of Heaven and Earth *(Final Perseverance)*

Angel of God

Angel of God, my guardian dear, to whom His love entrusts me here, ever this day be at my side to light and guard, to rule and guide. Amen.

Eternal Rest

Eternal rest grant to them, O Lord, and let perpetual light shine upon them. May they rest in peace. Amen.

The Sacraments

Baptism	Anointing of the Sick
Confirmation	Eucharist
Penance	Matrimony
Holy Orders	

The Great Commandments

1. You shall love the Lord your God
   with your whole heart,
   with your whole soul,
   and with all your mind.
2. You shall love your neighbor as yourself.

MT. 22:37-39

The Ten Commandments

1. I, the Lord, am your God. You shall not have other gods besides me.
2. You shall not take the name of the Lord, your God, in vain.
3. Remember to keep holy the sabbath day.
4. Honor your father and your mother.
5. You shall not kill.
6. You shall not commit adultery.
7. You shall not steal.
8. You shall not bear false witness against your neighbor.
9. You shall not covet your neighbor's wife.
10. You shall not covet anything that belongs to your neighbor.

The Beatitudes

1. How blest are the poor in spirit: the reign of God is theirs.
2. Blest too are the sorrowing; they shall be consoled.
3. [Blest are the lowly; they shall inherit the land.]
4. Blest are they who hunger and thirst for holiness;
   they shall have their fill.

5. Blest are they who show mercy; mercy shall be theirs.
6. Blest are the single-hearted for they shall see God.
7. Blest too the peacemakers; they shall be called sons of God.
8. Blest are those persecuted for holiness' sake; the reign of God is theirs. MT. 5:3-10

Some Duties of Catholic Christians *
(Precepts of the Church)

To keep holy the day of the Lord's Resurrection: to worship God by participating in Mass every Sunday and Holy Day of Obligation; to avoid those activities that would hinder renewal of soul and body, e.g., needless work and business activities, unnecessary shopping, etc.

To lead a sacramental life: to receive Holy Communion frequently and the sacrament of Penance regularly

—to receive the sacrament of Penance at least once a year (annual confession is obligatory only if serious sin is involved.)

—minimally, to receive Holy Communion at least once a year, between the first Sunday of Lent and Trinity Sunday.

To study Catholic teaching in preparation for the sacrament of Confirmation, to be confirmed, and then to continue to study and advance the cause of Christ.

° Taken from the Document, *Basic Teachings for Catholic Religious Education*, © 1973, National Conference of Catholic Bishops.

To observe the marriage laws of the Church: to give religious training (by example and word) to one's children; to use parish schools and religious education programs.

To strengthen and support the Church: one's own parish community and parish priests; the worldwide Church and the Holy Father.

To do penance, including abstaining from meat and fasting from food on the appointed days.

To join in the missionary spirit and apostolate of the Church.

Holy Days of Obligation in the United States

All Sundays of the year
January 1, The Solemnity of Mary, Mother of God
Ascension of Our Lord
August 15, The Assumption of the Blessed
    Virgin Mary
November 1, All Saints' Day
December 8, The Immaculate Conception
December 25, Christmas Day

The Theological Virtues

Faith   Hope   Love

The Cardinal Virtues

Prudence   Justice   Fortitude   Temperance

Spiritual Works of Mercy

Counsel the doubtful
Instruct the ignorant
Admonish the sinner
Comfort the sorrowful
Forgive injuries
Bear wrongs patiently
Pray for the living and the
    dead

Corporal Works of Mercy

Feed the hungry
Give drink to the thirsty
Clothe the naked
Shelter the homeless
Visit the sick
Visit the imprisoned
Bury the dead

The Gifts of the Holy Spirit

Wisdom
Understanding
Counsel
Fortitude

Knowledge
Piéty
Fear of the Lord

The Fruits of the Holy Spirit

Charity
Joy
Peace
Patience
Kindness
Goodness

Long-suffering
Humility
Fidelity
Modesty
Continence
Chastity

The Seven Capital Sins

Pride
Covetousness
Lust

Anger
Gluttony

Envy
Sloth

The Six Sins Against the Holy Spirit

1. Despair of one's salvation
2. Presumption of God's mercy
3. Resisting the known truth of faith
4. Envy of the graces received by others
5. Obstinacy in one's sins
6. Final impenitence

The Four Sins that Cry to Heaven for Vengeance

1. Voluntary murder
2. The sin of impurity against nature
3. Taking advantage of the poor
4. Defrauding the workingman of his wages

The Last Things

Death   Judgment   Heaven   Hell

How To Baptize in Case of Emergency

Pour ordinary water on the forehead of the person to be baptized, and say while pouring it:

"I baptize you in the name of the Father, and of the Son, and of the Holy Spirit."

N.B. Any person of either sex, who has reached the use of reason, can and should baptize in case of necessity; the same person must say the words while pouring the water.

How To Prepare for a Sick Call

Cover a small table with a white tablecloth. If possible, the table should be prepared near the bed so as to be within sight of the sick person. If customary, a vessel of holy water should be provided, as well as candles.

When the priest enters the house, he gives everyone a greeting of peace and then places the Blessed Eucharist on the table. All adore it. Then the priest sprinkles the sick person and the room with holy water, saying the prescribed prayer. The priest may then hear the sick person's confession. If sacramental confession is not part of the rite or if others are to receive communion along with the sick person, the priest invites them to join in a penitential rite. A text from Scripture may then be read by one of those present or by the priest, who may explain the text. The Lord's Prayer follows. Then the priest distributes Holy Communion. A period of sacred silence may be observed. A concluding prayer and a blessing complete the Rite of Communion of the Sick.

Sacrament of the Anointing of the Sick

We should call the priest in time when someone is in danger of death from sickness, accident or old age so that he may receive the grace and consolation from the Sacrament of Anointing of the Sick. In fact, Christ's minister should be called to visit the sick in any serious illness even when death does not seem near, because he will bring them the sacraments they need. Through His representative the divine Physician will come to the side of His suffering brother to be his strength and comfort.

Those who are in danger of death should be told of their condition so that they may prepare themselves to receive Christ in the sacraments worthily. It is false mercy to keep a very sick person ignorant of the fact that he may soon face God. Never wait until the person has lost consciousness or has gone into a coma before calling the priest.

In case of sudden or unexpected death, always call a priest, because absolution and the anointing can be given conditionally for some time after apparent death.

The elderly who are in a weakened condition are also encouraged by the Church to receive the Anointing of the Sick, even though no dangerous illness is present.

══ St. Paul Book & Media Centers ══

ALASKA
  750 West 5th Ave., Anchorage, AK 99501; 907-272-8183
CALIFORNIA
  3908 Sepulveda Blvd., Culver City, CA 90230; 310-397-8676
  5945 Balboa Ave., San Diego, CA 92111; 619-565-9181
  46 Geary Street, San Francisco, CA 94108; 415-781-5180
FLORIDA
  145 S.W. 107th Ave., Miami, FL 33174; 305-559-6715
HAWAII
  1143 Bishop Street, Honolulu, HI 96813; 808-521-2731
ILLINOIS
  172 North Michigan Ave., Chicago, IL 60601; 312-346-4228
LOUISIANA
  4403 Veterans Memorial Blvd., Metairie, LA 70006; 504-887-7631
MASSACHUSETTS
  50 St. Paul's Ave., Jamaica Plain, Boston, MA 02130; 617-522-8911
  Rte. 1, 885 Providence Hwy., Dedham, MA 02026; 617-326-5385
MISSOURI
  9804 Watson Rd., St. Louis, MO 63126; 314-965-3512
NEW JERSEY
  561 U.S. Route 1, Wick Plaza, Edison, NJ 08817; 908-572-1200
NEW YORK
  150 East 52nd Street, New York, NY 10022; 212-754-1110
  78 Fort Place, Staten Island, NY 10301; 718-447-5071
OHIO
  2105 Ontario Street (at Prospect Ave.), Cleveland, OH 44115;
  216-621-9427
PENNSYLVANIA
  214 W. DeKalb Pike, King of Prussia, PA 19406; 215-337-1882
SOUTH CAROLINA
  243 King Street, Charleston, SC 29401; 803-577-0175
TEXAS
  114 Main Plaza, San Antonio, TX 78205; 210-224-8101
VIRGINIA
  1025 King Street, Alexandria, VA 22314; 703-549-3806
GUAM
  285 Farenholt Avenue, Suite 308, Tamuning, Guam 96911;
  671-649-4377
CANADA
  3022 Dufferin Street, Toronto, Ontario, Canada M6B 3T5;
  416-781-9131; 1-800-668-2078

50¢   ISBN 0-8198-1133-5